KIM'S UNBREAKABLE SPIRIT:

The Truth Always Comes To The Light

by
Teresa Jones
for
Kim A. Porter

Dedicated to

all who have been impacted by

Kim in a positive way.

She lives on through your stories.

KIM'S UNBREAKABLE SPIRIT

KIM'S UNBREAKABLE SPIRIT

TABLE OF CONTENTS

KIM'S UNBREAKABLE SPIRIT

KIM'S UNBREAKABLE SPIRIT

INTRODUCTION

This book was not written to shame anyone. Neither was it published to be used in the court of law. The words were carefully chosen to inspire the reader. I want everyone to know they are not alone in their struggles. That no matter the darkness, everything becomes revealed.

It was written as a reminder that the truth always comes to light. Everything that has ever been done behind closed doors with malicious intent, eventually becomes known. No matter our status and what is achieved that can not be escaped. When we know that we begin to approach life in a different way. Knowing that the camera is on us at all times even when it appears it's not filming.

Something that I've learned throughout my journey is that we live eternally through stories. While our physical bodies may not live forever, the memories of us always seem to do. The impact we have made lives on far longer than we do. So let us all courageously live life to the fullest, treating everyone with love, respect, and the utmost kindness. Then when the sun shines as it always does, that is all that will ever be shown.

KIM'S UNBREAKABLE SPIRIT

KIM'S UNBREAKABLE SPIRIT

CHAPTER ONE
Your Worth

mani was about to graduate highschool with honors. All of the years of studying had finally paid off. Her father promised her that if she graduated with that prestige, his gift to her would be a car. Since Imani kept her promise he intended to do the same.

Imani's father was a wise man and wanted her daughter to be well prepared for the world. He had a lesson he was going to teach her with the car. On Imani's graduation day, he couldn't be more proud. Tears filled his eyes as he watched his only child walk across the stage. His wife passed away a few years ago so Imani was all he had. Each time he saw her smile it reminded him of his wife.

"Congratulations baby, I'm so proud of you" he said as he hugged her tight. "Thank you Daddy, I wouldn't be here without you, " she said with excitement. As promised, he gave her the keys to a car. The car was much older than she expected but Imani was still deeply grateful.

The father then told her before he gave it to her, that he wanted her to take it to the used car lot and tell them he wanted to sell it. The father wanted to see how much they would give her for it. The daughter obeyed and told the father they would only give $1,000 due to the car being worn out. The father then told her to take it to the pawn

shop and see if she gets a better deal there. Imani listened

and then said the pawn shop would only offer $100 because

the car was very old. He then said to put it online and the

offer was slightly less than the used car lot. The father

finally told his baby girl to go to a car club just to see out

of curiosity what they would offer.

By this time, Imani was getting slightly frustrated.

What was her father trying to teach her? Although hesitant,

she once again listened to her father. This time, Imani

opened the doors of their home with excitement. "Daddy,

you're not going to believe this, they wanted to give me

$100,000! They said it's because it's an iconic car and

collectors desire it!" she screamed with enthusiasm. Then the father shared with her what he wanted to share all along. He told her the right place will always value her according to her worth. And to never be angry if you're not valued, it only means you're not at the right place. Those who truly appreciate you will always value you highly. Never remain in a space where someone will not treat you according to your worth.

We've all been in situations where people have taken us for granted. Maybe the relationship started off with appreciation, but then eventually we became a doormat. Allowing them to walk all over us whenever they please. Thoughts cross your mind that maybe you deserve it.

I wanna tell you that you don't. You don't deserve to be taken for granted. Neither should you receive any type of abuse from anyone. If the partner you're with is not willing to treat you like the prized possession you are, I promise there are millions of others who would. But you're never going to realize that spending your entire life trying to get someone to acknowledge your value.

People from the outside see Kim only as a model and actress. They look at the appearance but are completely unaware of the value. All that is able to be offered as a strong, passionate, and supportive woman. Doing the best she can as a mother and even starting a lifestyle planning company in Atlanta for others with friends.

We can not get so caught up in lies about ourselves that we begin to believe them. Those thoughts of deserving mistreatment must always be immediately removed. As Tony Robbins said "We have to divorce the lies and marry the truth." It's time to reclaim your power and remember what's true about you. You are strong and have unbelievable value. Always know your worth.

KIM'S UNBREAKABLE SPIRIT

KIM'S UNBREAKABLE SPIRIT

CHAPTER TWO
Manipulation

D estiny was a single woman of 25. She just started a career in the bank industry and was excited for life. Destiny had a strong routine every morning. She would wake up, read her bible, go to the gym, meditate, listen to empowering podcasts, and go to church every Sunday. Her routine helped keep her strong mentally and emotionally.

While she was out with friends at a club one night, she met a charming man by the name of Tony. There was an instant attraction and they danced the night away. Song after song the moments became even more heated as they held one another tightly. Her hands firmly on his shoulders while his hands gripping her waist. After a fun night of drinks and dancing, it was time to go home. Tony asked for her number afterwards and she gladly gave it to him.

Destiny soon learned that Tony had his own business. He had been a bachelor for years and seemed like he was ready to settle down. Sometime afterwards they began talking regularly and it eventually evolved into a relationship.

Everything started off wonderful in Destiny's eyes. They were inseperable. Phone conversations would sometimes last for hours and she could tell him anything.

She felt everything was perfect. This may be the man of her dreams she thought. Destiny's routine had even begun to change and she found herself not doing the things she would usually do daily before starting her day.

As time went on, she began to notice some red flags about Tony. He started to become very controlling over her. Tony never wanted Destiny to see her friends and family. He had to know her whereabouts at every moment and if he didn't, he would blow up her phone with text messages and call until she finally responded. This went on for a couple of years. It wasn't until a childhood friend from out of town was visiting, and insisted on catching up with Destiny while she was there, that things began to change.

When they met up her friend could immediately sense something was wrong. Finally, Destiny decided to tell her everything without holding anything back. Tears filled her eyes as she began to confide in her friend all that she had been experiencing. She just wanted to be happy and couldn't understand how she got herself into such a toxic situation. Her friend told her to end the relationship immediately and come live with her. Destiny listened and eventually got back to feeling like herself again.

Does that story sound familiar to you? When everything seems to be perfect only to find out that it's not?

The foundation of having high self-esteem comes from our rituals. That daily routine you had when you were single. We must always remember to continue to do them because that is what keeps us grounded mentally. It's difficult to manipulate a strong mind; therefore we should always do what got it strong in the first place.

We know that feeling too well when there's a mutual attraction with someone. But it's important to not get so caught up in our feelings for the person that we begin to neglect our well-being. Because that's the beginning of becoming more susceptible to manipulation. It's the invitation to being in abusive relationships far longer than you should've ever had. It also leads to us lying to others about how we feel when truthfully, we're hurting but want everything to seem like it's fine. It is not fine. You matter and deserve so much more. Your sense of being matters and your feelings are valid. So I need you to go back to your strong routines and if you've never had one, it's time to create one. Being strong minded gives us discernment. So no matter how sweet and charming someone may be, we will still be able to see their true colors. So start today. You got this girl!

KIM'S UNBREAKABLE SPIRIT

CHAPTER THREE

Truth Shall Come to The Light

Luke 12:2-3

"God says that secrets will be uncovered, the truth will come forth, and God's thought about every behavior and action will be vindicated."

Luke 8:17

"For all that is secret will eventually be brought into the open, and everything that is concealed will be brought to light and made known to all."

Abriannah had been married for over 10 years. She had a husband and 3 beautiful children. Her life seemed like a fairy tale. Family vacations every year. They would travel the world together. She was in a career she was passionate about. Life seemed like it couldn't be better.

Until one day, she came home early from work and caught her man with another woman. Abriannah was devastated. She couldn't believe what she saw with her very eyes. Not her marriage. How could this happen to her? The husband jumped out of bed and told her she was sorry but Abriannah was speechless. After giving it some thought, she finally made the decision to get therapy with her husband.

However one night, she overheard her husband talking to a friend over the phone. The husband told the friend that he knew she wasn't leaving because he's the real breadwinner. Where would she go? Abriannah made the toughest decision she ever had to make at that moment, she decided to leave him. It was a tough journey in the beginning but she was able to get through it and find love once again.

There used to be a time when people could do whatever they wanted with no consequences. Because of their status in life no one would dare challenge them. Those times have greatly changed. As we've seen on the news whether it's been Harvey Weinstein or Bill Cosby, everything eventually comes to light.

It's inspiring men and women from all over to be more mindful of how we treat one another. Reminding us we all are human no matter our financial status. And we should be treated according to human value, not what's currently in our bank accounts. This is how we become an example for the next generation. It's how we influence our sons and daughters to become great men and women. Perhaps it's how we get closer to what God wanted us to be all along. Mighty men and women that make his heart rejoice.

I don't know about you but I'm embracing that. I remember telling a friend years ago that if we're always focusing on attempting to do the right thing, then we will never have to worry about being caught doing the wrong thing. I want to end this chapter with words from American memoirist and poet Maya Angelou, "Just do right. Right may not be expedient, it may not be profitable, but it will satisfy your soul. It brings you the kind of protection that bodyguards can't give you. So try to live your life in a way that you will not regret years of useless virtue, inertia, and timidity.

Take up the battle. Take it up. It's yours.

This is your life.

This is your world.

33

KIM'S UNBREAKABLE SPIRIT

CHAPTER FOUR
Unbreakable

"You can kill my body, and you can take my life, but you can never kill my soul. My soul will live forever!"

Huey Newton

Those were the last words of the co-founder Black Panther Huey Newton. I'm not able to comment about someone's soul living forever, but I can say people still talk about him until this very day. So if the objective was to end his life and all conversation about Huey

Newton, his murderer failed. I want you to know that you are stronger than you realize. And no matter what you go through, your spirit is unbreakable.

Nevaeh and her partner were both martial artists. They had been running a martial arts program for years. On the outside, it seemed like they were the perfect couple. They always received the greatest compliments from their students. However, behind closed doors, Nevaeh was the most miserable she had ever been in her whole life.

For over six years Nevaeh had been experiencing physical, mental, emotional, and even financial abuse from him. She felt defeated and broken. She wanted the world for her daughter but didn't know how to get out of this situation.

Nevaeh became an expert at hiding her pain. She successfully created a double life that everyone wished they had. But the truth was catching up with her. The depression she experienced daily only seemed to get more intense. She just didn't think anyone would believe her. Someone who had such a high profile in the martial arts community could never allow themselves to be in such a situation she thought.

She felt alone. From being physically abused while she was pregnant, being called fat, stupid, and that she would never amount to anything. Nevaeh thought this just may be her life. She gave up on all of her dreams because she had no support. Everything seemed hopeless for her.

It wasn't until she had an epiphany one night that things began to change. She began to think about what might happen to her daughter if she stayed. The trauma she would grow up having if she didn't make some changes. Her baby was everything to her and she knew she had to make a decision then.

Finally, Nevaeh got her daughter, belongings, and left one night while her partner was working. Her first night leaving was horrible because they had nowhere to stay. They walked the streets with a garbage of clothes and toys and finally went to sleep on a bench. This went on for several weeks.

Eventually she learned about Women Against Abuse. She began calling the hotline several times a day to find a bed at one of their safe havens. A sense of relief came over her as she and her daughter walked through the doors of the safe haven. She could finally let her guard down and think with a clarity of mind.

Nevaeh was ready to take her life back because for years it felt like she had given it away. She had to forgive herself for staying in the relationship so long. She also had to erase all the lies about what her partner said she couldn't do by proving him wrong and doing them. All of the experiences she had of being homeless, broken, and defeated molded her. She became an incredible coach, speaker and advocate. She even won her first world title during all the positive changes she made for herself. Neveah is in a healthy relationship now and is closer than ever to her daughter after the experiences they had together.

Stories like these are what define us. Having those breaking points and coming out victorious on the other side. Just when the abuser or manipulator thought they could win, we gain our strength and confidence back. We begin to value ourselves again and know we deserve better. We make tough decisions even though they may be uncomfortable in the beginning. You are unbreakable. No matter how many times someone has tried to break your spirit they will not succeed. You have so much to offer the world and the sooner you remember that, the sooner your life becomes exciting. I'm going to end this chapter with words from Oprah Winfrey. "Life is about finding yourself, embracing your strengths and weaknesses, and being true to who you are."

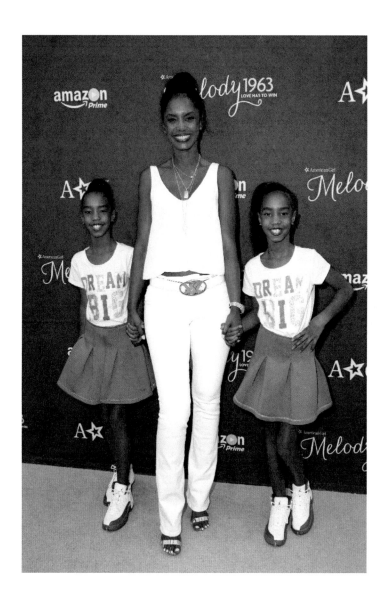

KIM'S UNBREAKABLE SPIRIT

KIM'S LEGACY

Kimberly Antwinette Porter was born on December 15th 1970 in Columbus, Georgia. She passed away at the young age of 47 in Los Angeles, California. She was a model, actress and entrepreneur. She had 4 children of which one was with singer-songwriter Al B. Sure! The others were with entrepreneur Sean Combs. She appeared in a few films and numerous music videos. She also founded The Three Brown Girls (A Lifestyle Planning Company) with friends Nicole Cooke-Johnson and Eboni

Elektra. She along with the company helped start singer Janelle Monáes career in the music industry. Janelle has been forever grateful to Kim for believing in her. Kim's legacy will live on through her kids, but it will also live on through anyone she impacted. If anyone had the pleasure of seeing Kim's smile in person they were destined to have a great day. We will always remember you Kim and miss you. Keep smiling!

Made in the USA
Las Vegas, NV
24 October 2024

10442995R00036